Grace Johnson

Fast Day Cookery or Meals Without Meat

Grace Johnson

Fast Day Cookery or Meals Without Meat

ISBN/EAN: 9783744796644

Printed in Europe, USA, Canada, Australia, Japan

Cover: Foto ©Lupo / pixelio.de

More available books at **www.hansebooks.com**

FAST-DAY COOKERY

OR

MEALS WITHOUT MEAT

BY

GRACE JOHNSON

AUTHORESS OF "ANGLO-INDIAN AND ORIENTAL COOKERY"

LONDON
GRIFFITH FARRAN & CO.

NEWBERY HOUSE, 39 CHARING CROSS ROAD
1893

PREFACE

ENCOURAGED by the kindly manner in which the Press has dealt with my " Anglo-Indian and Oriental Cookery," and at the repeated request of friends, I am writing this little book.

In its compilation, I have had in view both the Anglican and Roman communions.

There are many who keep the Fasts and Abstinences prescribed by their Church, and there are many more who would do so if their food was served up and cooked in a healthy way. As a rule, fish and vegetables are very little understood in this country, and even in the houses of the better class one sees little else than the eternal boiled and fried fish. As to vegetables, they are out of it altogether. If this be the case where money is no object, how much harder is it for those who are obliged to make the most of everything?

I do not pretend to teach in this little book, only to give a few novel and useful recipes that most housewives will find really good and economical, and also to show that a non-flesh diet can be and is both healthy and appetising.

The book will be found useful by others than those for whom it is specially written, and most of the recipes will be practicable at all times of the year.

A word in conclusion to the careful housewife in getting tinned fish. Always get the *best* brand; it is not wise to go in for cheap goods in this line.

I cannot speak too highly of Edwards' Desiccated Soups. They make delicious soups of themselves, and in conjunction with other things they have no equal. Their tomato is simply invaluable; I would not be without it for anything.

To those who find pastry indigestible I would recommend them to try "Coombs' Eureka Flour"; it makes delicious pastry, and requires no baking powder, and it has the advantage of being thoroughly digestible.

I have mentioned how to use all these in most of the recipes. I have not made any pretence to make this what is called a high-class cookery book; my aim and object is to bring it within the range of most people, while many of the dishes are good enough for any high-class table, and would be found a welcome and novel addition.

GRACE JOHNSON.

FAST-DAY COOKERY.

SOUPS.

1. Oyster Soup.

OPEN one dozen oysters, preserve the liquor.

Put into a pan two ounces of butter, with an onion and one bead of garlic chopped very fine ; let these cook till they are a golden colour, then add one and a half pints of milk, and one and a half pints of water, and the liquor of the oysters, twelve cloves, twelve peppercorns, three bay-leaves, salt and pepper to taste. Stir in a bowl three ounces of fine florador to the consistence of cream, and when the soup comes to a boil, stir it in, and then let it boil for about ten minutes. Let it simmer after this very gently for half an hour, strain through a wire sieve, then add the oysters, a grate of nutmeg, the peel of a lemon grated ; let it simmer for twenty minutes. Serve hot.

2. Lobster Soup.

Cut up an onion into thin rings, chop two beads of garlic, and fry these a golden brown in two ounces of butter, with twenty-four cloves, twelve peppercorns, and three bay-leaves. Add one and a half pints of water, let it simmer gently for half an hour, then add two packets of Edwards' Desiccated White Soup; let it simmer half an hour longer, and strain. Then add either one pint of milk, or sixpence worth of cream, the rind of a lemon grated, quarter of a nutmeg grated, salt and pepper to taste; put it on the fire to warm through. Well pound the flesh of a fresh lobster, or the *very best* brand of tinned lobster, and pass it through a wire sieve into the soup, stir well, and thoroughly heat it. Serve with fried bread cut into small dice shape.

---

3. Scallop Soup.

Cut up an onion into rings, two beads of garlic, and fry in two ounces of butter a golden colour. Add one and a half pints of water, the same of milk, twenty-four cloves, twelve peppercorns, a sprig of tarragon, three bay-leaves, a stick of celery, two-penny packet of Edwards' White Soup; let them simmer for one hour.

Chop up about half a dozen scallops, strain the soup through a wire sieve, add the scallops, pepper and salt to taste, and a grate of lemon peel. Serve very hot with fried bread cut into little dice.

4. Cockle Soup.

Cut up an onion into thin rings, and chop two beads of garlic, fry in two ounces of butter with twenty-four cloves a delicate brown, then add two tablespoons of tarragon vinegar, two tablespoons mushroom ketchup, two teaspoons of Chili vinegar, and three pints of water; thicken with two ounces of flour that has been rubbed smooth in a bowl to the consistence of cream; then add a stick of celery, a pinch of thyme, parsley, basil and sage. Let these simmer for one hour; add pepper and salt to taste, and strain through a sieve. Lastly, add one pint of *picked* cockles, with their liquor. Serve hot.

5. Eel Soup.

Boil two pounds of eels, that have been skinned and cleaned, in two quarts of water. Add a bunch of sweet herbs, two-penny packet of Edwards' White Soup, one onion stuck with cloves, two beads of garlic, two ounces of butter, pepper and salt to taste, one small tea-cup of tomato conserve. Let it simmer gently for one hour, strain through a sieve, take the flesh of the fish off the bones, pass it through a sieve into the soup. Serve hot, with nicely toasted bread cut into neat pieces.

6. Haddock Soup.

Boil a smoked haddock in about three pints of water,
add to it an onion cut into quarters, two beads of garlic,
twenty-four cloves, a stick of cinnamon, a blade of maize,
a bunch of sweet herbs, twelve peppercorns; boil gently
for one hour; strain through a wire sieve, bone the fish, and
remove the skin, pass the flesh through the sieve into the
soup, thicken with half a penny packet of pea flour, rubbed
smooth in a little water, add a little tomato pulp if liked,
and two ounces of butter. Serve hot with fried bread cut
into dice.

7. Skate Soup.

Well skin and wash two pounds of skate—the cheaper parts
are the best for soup—boil in three pints of water for about
two hours very gently.

Cut up an onion into thin rings, chop two beads of garlic,
and fry in two ounces of butter a delicate golden colour;
now add the soup to this with one pint of milk, three bay-
leaves, twelve cloves, a blade of mace, and a stick of cinnamon, pepper and salt to taste. Let it simmer for half an
hour, strain through a wire sieve, take the meat of the fish,
and put neat pieces of it in the soup. Serve hot with toasted
bread cut into neat pieces.

8. Cod Soup.

Take a cod's head and shoulders, boil it gently in two quarts of water for one and a half hours.

Cut up an onion into rings, chop two beads of garlic, and fry in two ounces of butter and twenty-four cloves a nice brown, then add the fish liquor, three bay-leaves, a bunch of sweet herbs, pepper and salt to taste; thicken the soup with one packet of pea flour rubbed smooth in a bowl with a little water, stir well, then add one teaspoon of Chili vinegar, one tablespoon of tarragon vinegar, and one tablespoon of mushroom ketchup; strain, and serve with fried bread cut into dice.

9. Salt Herring Mullagatawny.

Cut up an onion into rings, chop three beads of garlic, fry in two ounces of butter with twenty-four cloves a nice brown, then add one tablespoon of the best currie powder, stir, then put in two quarts of water. Cut up three red herrings, salted ones, into pieces, add it to the rest; let it simmer gently one hour; strain, put it back into the pan, and add two packets of Edwards' Tomato Soup, and three bay-leaves. Take the nicest bits of the fish, free from skin and bone, and put them in the soup; let it simmer an hour longer, take out the bay-leaves, and serve with a separate dish of boiled rice.

10. Welk Soup.

Cut up an onion into thin rings, chop two beads of garlic, fry in two ounces of butter with twenty-four cloves a nice brown, add two quarts of water and one quart of welks, picked, three bay-leaves, a bunch of sweet herbs, a carrot cut into thin slices, a turnip cut into thin slices, and a few sticks of celery chopped small. Boil gently for two hours; strain, pulp the vegetables through a sieve, and return the soup and vegetables into the pan. Add one packet of Edwards' Tomato Soup, pepper and salt to taste; simmer for half an hour. Serve hot with toasted bread cut into dice. The welks can be eaten with vinegar, pepper, and salt, separately, if liked.

---

11. Bread Soup.

Boil two large onions in one pint of water, with twenty-four cloves, and a blade of mace, and twenty-four pepper-corns. Let it boil till the onions are quite soft, then pass it through a sieve. Add two pints of milk, half a pound of bread crumbs passed through a sieve, pepper and salt to taste, and two ounces of butter; stir, let it come to the boil, and serve.

12. Onion Soup.

Boil one pound of onions till quite soft. Pass them through a sieve, mix with them two ounces of butter, three pints of milk, and pepper and salt to taste.

13. Pea Soup.

Boil one pint of the best peas in two quarts of water and a mite of soda till they are quite soft. If the peas get too thick add a little more water; when quite soft, pass them through a sieve into a nice *purée*. Cut up an onion in thin rings, then chop it *very* small, also two beads of garlic, fry in two ounces of butter a golden brown. Then add twenty-four cloves, a carrot cut into thin slices, and a turnip cut into thin slices, and the *purée;* let it simmer gently till the carrot and turnip are soft, and then again strain it. Add pepper and salt to taste. Serve with dried powdered mint, and fried bread cut into dice.

14. Green Pea Soup.

Boil one pint of dried green peas in two quarts of water with a mite of soda till the peas are quite soft. If the water evaporates add a little more; pass the peas through a wire sieve. Now chop up an onion *very* small, also two beads of garlic, fry in two ounces of butter a golden colour. Add your peas, then a whole carrot, a whole turnip, and two sticks of celery; simmer gently till the vegetables are soft, remove the vegetables, add pepper and salt to taste, and serve the *purée* with dry powdered mint and fried bread cut into dice.

15. Turnip Soup.

Boil four large turnips till quite tender. Pass them through a sieve, add three pints of milk and put them on one side, cut up an onion into rings, chop two beads of garlic, and fry in two ounces of butter a gold colour. Add twelve cloves, twelve peppercorns, a piece of green ginger, and three bay-leaves. Then put in your turnip *purée,* pepper and salt to taste. Simmer gently for half an hour; strain and serve.

16. Vegetable Marrow Soup.

Boil a vegetable marrow till quite tender. Pass it through a sieve, add pepper and salt to taste, and three pints of milk. Warm it up thoroughly and melt into it two ounces of butter. Serve with toast cut into nice shapes,

17. Potato Soup.

Cut up an onion into rings, chop two beads of garlic, fry and add two ounces of butter a nice golden colour, add twelve cloves, twelve peppercorns, three bay-leaves, one carrot cut into slices, one turnip cut into slices, a stick or two of celery chopped, one pound of potatoes peeled and cut into slices, and one quart of water and one quart of milk. Boil gently till all the vegetables are tender enough; pass them through a sieve; if the *purée* is too thick add a little more milk; warm up thoroughly. Add pepper and salt to taste, and serve with fried bread cut into dice.

18. Haricot Bean Soup.

Boil a half pint of haricots in two quarts of water, with a mite of soda, one onion, one carrot, one turnip, two sticks of celery chopped. When quite tender pass all through a sieve. Add two ounces of butter, pepper and salt to taste, and two tablespoons of tomato conserve. Serve with fried bread cut in dice.

19. Lentil Soup.

Boil one pint of lentils in two quarts of water to a pulp. Cut up an onion, chop two beads of garlic, and fry in two

B

ounces of butter with twenty-four cloves a nice gold colour. Add the lentils to this, put in salt to taste, and just before serving a squeeze of lemon juice.

20. German Lentil Soup.

Boil one pint of German lentils in two quarts of water, with a mite of soda. When quite soft pass through a wire sieve ; stir into the *purée* two ounces of butter, pepper and salt to taste. Serve with fried bread cut into dice.

21. Tomato Puree.

Cut up an onion into rings, chop two beads of garlic, and fry a pale brown in two ounces of butter. Add twenty-four cloves, and two pounds of tomatoes cut up in quarters. Let it simmer gently till the tomatoes are quite soft ; strain through a sieve. Add one pint of water, pepper and salt to taste ; let it boil up, and put in a tablespoon of butter rolled in as much flour as it will take up ; stir well. A few drops of tarragon vinegar are a great improvement.

22. Mixed Vegetable Soup.

Boil in two quarts of water a turnip cut up, a carrot cut up, three sticks of celery cut up, two leeks, and a small cauliflower cut into sprigs. Boil till quite soft. Pass it all through a sieve. Cut up an onion, chop two beads of garlic, and fry in two ounces of butter a pale golden colour. Add your vegetable *purée*, and pepper and salt to taste. Serve with fried bread cut into dice.

---

23. Florador Soup.

Cut up an onion into rings, chop up two beads of garlic, fry in two ounces of butter with twenty-four cloves a nice gold colour. Add three pints of milk; let it boil up very slowly. Have ready a quarter of a pound of fine florador, mixed with almost one pint of cold milk, nice and smooth like cream. Add this to the boiling milk; stir all the time, so that it does not stick or get lumpy. Let it get thick, and strain. Just before serving add a few drops of tarragon vinegar.

---

24. Barley Soup.

Cut up an onion into rings and chop fine, chop two beads of garlic, and fry in two ounces of butter a golden brown. Add two quarts of water, three ounces of pearl barley, one carrot cut into slices, a turnip cut into slices, three sticks of celery chopped; boil till the barley is quite tender. Add pepper and salt to taste, a few drops of tarragon

2 FAST-DAY COOKERY.

vinegar, a few drops of clove vinegar, and a tablespoon of mushroom ketchup. Serve with toast cut into neat pieces.

25. Mullagatawny Soup.

Cut up an onion into thin rings, chop two beads of garlic, and fry in two ounces of butter a golden brown, with twenty-four cloves; then add one tablespoon of the best of currie powder; fry a minute; add three pints of water. Rub smooth with a little water one packet of pea flour; add this to the boiling soup. Now add one penny packet of Edwards' Tomato Soup; let it simmer gently for half an hour; just before serving add the juice of half a lemon, and salt to taste. Serve with a separate dish of boiled rice.

26. Spinach Puree.

Clean, wash, and pick two pounds of spinach. Put it in a pan with one pint of water, boil till it is quite soft, pass it all through a sieve, add three ounces of butter, and pepper and salt to taste. If the *purée* is too thick, add a little more warm water. Serve with fried bread cut into dice. This is a very simple but delicious *purée*.

27. Sorrel Puree.

Clean, pick, and wash two pounds of sorrel. Cut up an onion into rings, chop two beads of garlic, and fry in three ounces of butter a golden colour. Now add the sorrel. Let it get quite soft, and pass it through a wire sieve, liquor and all; add as much hot water as will make the *purée* a nice consistence for soup. Pepper and salt to taste. Serve with fried bread cut into dice.

28. Artichoke Puree.

Peel two pounds of Jerusalem artichokes, and boil them till quite soft. Pass them through a wire sieve; add three pints of milk; let it come to the boil, then add three ounces of butter. Pepper and salt to taste. Serve with fried bread. This is a delicious soup, and very nutritious.

29. Carrot Puree.

Scrape and wash four large carrots; cut them into quarters, and boil till quite soft; pass them through a sieve; cut up an onion into rings; chop up two beads of garlic, and fry these with twenty-four cloves a nice brown in two ounces of butter; then add the carrot *purée*, two and a half pints of water, three bay-leaves, a stick of cinnamon, a blade of mace, one packet of Edwards' White Soup. Pepper and salt to taste. Let it simmer gently for an hour. Strain again, and serve with fried bread cut into dice. A few drops of tarragon is an improvement.

30. Pearl Sago Soup.

Boil a quarter pound of pearl sago in two quarts of water till quite clear, and as thick as possible; then add two packets of Edwards' Tomato Soup, one onion stuck with cloves, a roll of lemon peel, two white beads of garlic, three bay-leaves, and three ounces of butter. Simmer gently for one hour. Before serving remove the onion, garlic, peel, and bay-leaves. Add a few drops of tarragon vinegar, one tablespoon of Worcester sauce, and two of mushroom ketchup, salt and pepper to taste.

N.B.—I have made some of these soups very thick on purpose, so that there may be more substance in them. They can, moreover, be made thinner or thicker as desired by either omitting or adding hot water.

SAUCES.

I GIVE but few, but these are novel to a certain extent. The white butter sauce alone can be varied in many ways, either savoury or sweet. If for sweets, the salt and savouries left out, and sugar and flavouring as desired put to it. Any cook with very little trouble can do this, and it does not require extraordinary skill to vary these sauces according to what is required.

1. White Butter Sauce.

Put into a pan half a pint of milk, with two ounces of butter; let it gradually come to the boil.

Have ready a tablespoon of flour rubbed down in a little cold milk. Add this to the boiling milk, stir, and let it thicken, add salt to taste. This is more delicate than the ordinary melted butter.

2. Onion Sauce.

Boil two large onions, stick two or three cloves into them. When quite soft, pass them through a wire sieve, and add the pulp to a sauce, as No. 1.

23

3. Parsley and Butter Sauce.

Pick some parsley in neat bunches, wash and clear of grit, dry thoroughly in a cloth, chop *very* fine, and add about two tablespoons to the sauce No. 1. Let it simmer very gently for a few minutes till the parsley is cooked; stir occasionally, that it does not burn or get lumpy.

4. Egg Sauce.

Boil two eggs for ten minutes, then throw them in cold water; shell and chop fine; add to sauce No. 1. A little Nepaul pepper is an improvement. .

5. Sauce Piquant.

Cut up a small onion, chop two beads of garlic, and fry in two ounces of butter with twelve cloves, twelve peppercorns, and three bay-leaves. Add half a pint of milk. Let it slowly come to the boil.

Have ready one tablespoon of flour mixed smooth with a little cold milk, stir into the boiling milk, strain, let it cool a little; now add the yolk of an egg well beaten, a little Nepaul pepper and salt to taste. And lastly, chop up some tarragon and a little chervil that has been soaked in vinegar for a week previously. Add this *very* carefully, a little at a time, so that the sauce does not curdle. This sauce is a great favourite.

---

6. Bread Sauce.

Boil a small onion till very tender, pass it through a sieve; add to it half a pint of milk, two tablespoons of bread crumbs passed through a sieve, two ounces of butter, a few peppercorns, and salt to taste.

---

7. Celery Sauce.

Cut up the white part of a head of celery very small. Boil in just enough water to get it quite soft. Then add to this two tablespoons of cream, two ounces of butter, and a little flour mixed smooth in some cold milk, just to thicken it, salt to taste. Some like a little grated lemon peel and nutmeg.

---

8. Oyster Sauce.

Chop up half a dozen oysters and mix them with their liquor with sauce No. 1—a little grated nutmeg and lemon peel added.

---

9. Shrimp Sauce.

Pick and clean one pint of pink shrimps. Mix them with sauce No. 1.

10. Lemon Sauce.

Sauce No. 1. When a little cool, add the yolk of an egg well beaten, the rind of half a lemon grated, a pinch of Nepaul pepper and nutmeg.

11. Anchovy and Butter Sauce.

Sauce No. 1, with the addition of enough Anchovy sauce to flavour nicely, and a pinch of Nepaul pepper.

12. Jerusalem Artichoke Sauce.

Sauce No. 1, with half a pound of artichokes boiled till tender and passed through a sieve, added to it a good pinch of Nepaul pepper.

13. Brown Onion Sauce.

Chop up an onion very small, also one bead of garlic. Fry these in three ounces of butter, with one tablespoon of flour, till it is quite brown. Add half a pint of water, stir, and boil it up for about ten or fifteen minutes. Strain, and add pepper and salt to taste, and a little mushroom ketchup.

14. Piquant Brown Sauce.

Cut up an onion into rings ; chop up two beads of garlic. Fry these in three ounces of butter and a tablespoon of flour till quite brown. Add rather less than half a pint of water, two tablespoons of vinegar, one tablespoon of tarragon vinegar, one tablespoon of chervil, one tablespoon of clove, salt to taste, and a pinch of Nepaul pepper. Strain and serve.

15. Tomato Sauce.

Cut up a small onion into thin rings, chop a bead of garlic, and fry in two ounces of butter a pale yellow. Cut up three good-sized tomatoes, and let it all simmer together till quite soft. Pass it all through a fine wire sieve. Add enough water to make half a pint of sauce. Thicken with a little butter rolled in flour. Salt to taste and a few drops of tarragon vinegar.

16. Mushroom Sauce.

Cut up a very small onion, chop one bead of garlic, and fry in three ounces of butter, to which add a tablespoon of flour. Fry till brown. Add half a pint of water, stir, and let it thicken. Strain. Add salt and Nepaul pepper to taste, and about six good-sized mushrooms that have been peeled and picked and chopped. Let it simmer for about ten minutes very gently, and just before serving add a tablespoon of mushroom ketchup and a squeeze of lemon.

17. Brown Lemon.

Cut up an onion into rings; chop up two beads of garlic. Fry in three ounces of butter, with one tablespoon of flour, a nice brown. Add half a pint of water, let it thicken, and then strain it. Add the grated peel of half a lemon, the juice of a whole one, and salt and Nepaul pepper to taste.

18. Brown Parsley.

Cut up an onion into thin rings, chop two beads of garlic, and fry in three ounces of butter, with a tablespoon of flour, till quite brown. Add half a pint of water, let it thicken, and strain. Then add two tablespoons of finely chopped green parsley, salt and Nepaul pepper to taste.

19. Cocoa-nut Sauce.

Cut up an onion into thin rings, chop two beads of garlic, also two bay-leaves; fry these in three ounces of butter with twelve cloves and a tablespoon of flour; let it get quite brown. Add the milk of a cocoa-nut and enough water to make it half a pint; let it thicken, and strain, then add two tablespoons of scraped cocoa-nuts, salt and Nepaul pepper to taste. This is very good with boiled fish.

20. Beet-root Sauce.

Cut up an onion into rings, chop one head of garlic, fry in three ounces of butter with one tablespoon of flour. Add somewhat less than half a pint of water, two tablespoons of vinegar, one of tarragon vinegar, one of chervil vinegar, one teaspoon of Chili vinegar, and salt to taste. Strain, and then add to it a small beet-root passed through a wire sieve.

FISH IN VARIOUS WAYS.

I HAVE not given recipes for plain boiling and frying ; most cooks know how to do this perfectly well, and it would only be repeating what is in other books. I will only add that most of the sauces poured over plain boiled fish seem to change its character entirely ; for instance, boiled fillets of skate smothered in onion sauce taste very much like white meat. Some of the brown sauces, too, poured over good firm fleshed fish, seem very much like chicken or rabbit.

I have put all the fish recipes together, both those suited to *entrées* and the more substantial. I have done this because it is rather a difficult matter to arrange how the different dishes are to be served. Some are quite content with an *entrée* after the soup ; others want something more substantial to take the place of the usual joint ; they can, however, have fish pies, baked fish, boiled fish, fried fish, etc., which answer the purpose very well, and the lighter dishes can be used as *entrées*, and some even as savouries. A dinner of four or five courses can easily be had from these recipes.

1. Eel Pie.

Clean and skin two pounds of eels; cut them into pieces two inches in length, put them in a pie dish thus: a layer of fish, then sliced onions, a few cloves, and sliced tomatoes, some sliced hard-boiled eggs, and so on till the dish is full. Mix some salt and Nepaul pepper to taste, in a little warm water, say a *small* tea-cup; pour it over the fish. Cover with a nice crust either light or short, and bake a nice brown. Serve with a nice frill round the dish.

This is a very substantial and delicious dish. The short crust is more digestible and satisfying than the light, but this is a matter of individual taste.

2. Eel Stew.

Clean and skin two pounds of eels; cut them into two-inch pieces. Chop one onion and two heads of garlic very small, fry in three ounces of butter with one tablespoon of flour till it is a nice brown; add half a pint of water and let it thicken; strain, then add the eels to the sauce. One tablespoon of tarragon vinegar, one tablespoon of cloves, one tablespoon of chervil, Nepaul pepper and salt to taste, the grated rind of half a lemon, and a little grated nutmeg. A few turned olives and button mushrooms considerably improve it, but where expense is an object these may be left out.

3. Salt Fish and Egg Pie:

Get a good dry salt fish about three pounds. Soak it all night in water, then put it in the oven till soft enough to handle, remove all skin and bone, and make into nice large flakes ; put a layer of this in a pie dish, then a layer of sliced onions, a few cloves, a sprinkling of lemon thyme, some sliced hard-boiled eggs, and so on till the dish is full. Now mix half a cup of water with half a cup of good thick tomato conserve, add Nepaul pepper to it to taste ; pour it over the pie, and cover with either a light or a short crust, and bake a nice brown.

4. Salt Fish and Potato Pie.

Treat the fish as in previous recipe. Peel and boil two pounds of potatoes, mash them thoroughly, and mix them with the fish. Three hard-boiled eggs chopped fine, one tablespoon of chopped onion, three ounces of butter, and a teaspoon of herbs as for veal stuffing. Mix all thoroughly together, then put it in a well-greased pie dish, smooth it down, and score it with a fork, put a few dabs of butter over it here and there, and bake a nice brown.

5. Haddock and Potato.

Get a good sized smoked haddock; put it in the oven for a few minutes till it is cooked enough to handle, remove the skin and bone, flake it, and mix it with mashed potatoes, three ounces of butter, the grated peel of half a lemon, a little lemon thyme, some grated nutmeg, and salt and Nepaul pepper to taste. Put it in a greased pie dish; smooth the top, and score it with a fork, and bake a nice brown.

----

6. Skate Fricassee.

Cut up an onion into rings, chop one bead of garlic, fry in two ounces of butter with twelve cloves and two bay-leaves, a pale yellow. Add half a pint of milk, draw it aside, and let the milk cook very gently ten minutes; strain. Now mix smooth a tablespoon of flour with a little cold milk; pour it into the other just as it is boiling up; stir till it thickens. Add one pound of filleted skate, the grated rind of half a lemon, a grated nutmeg; let it cook gently till the fish is done. When a little cool, *i.e.*, when it is off the boil, add the yolk of an egg well beaten, and salt and Nepaul pepper to taste. Stir well, and thoroughly warm it, taking care the egg does not curdle; it is best to put the pan into a larger one containing hot water; this prevents the curdling of the egg. Serve this with a dish of mashed potatoes, or potato snow. It is a delicate and delicious dish and, skate being very nutritious, it is well suited for an invalid.

---

7. Skate Stew (Brown).

Cut up an onion into thin rings, chop two beads of garlic, and fry, in three ounces of butter with one tablespoon of flour and twelve cloves, a nice brown, quite a rich colour, then add half a pint of water, a blade of mace, a stick of cinnamon, the grated rind of half a lemon, three bay-leaves; stir, and let it thicken well, then add two tablespoons of mushroom ketchup, Nepaul pepper and salt to taste ; let it simmer very gently for half an hour ; strain, put it back in the pan, and add one pound of nicely crimped skate to the sauce ; let the fish cook very gently until done, which will take from twenty minutes to half an hour. Serve with sippets of fried bread and parsley round the dish.

---

8. Brown Oyster Stew.

Make the sauce just the same as in preceding recipe, only add the juice of the oysters to it ; strain, and add the oysters themselves. A few drops of tarragon and Chili vinegar are an improvement, and the juice of half a lemon. This is a delicate dish, and much liked.

---

9. Lobster Cutlets.

Well pound the flesh of a good fresh lobster in a mortar (the best brand of tin lobster will answer as well), mix with it about two ounces of butter, one small cup of bread crumbs, salt and Nepaul pepper to taste, the grated rind of a lemon and half a nutmeg grated, mix all together with two well beaten eggs; form into cutlet shapes, and egg and bread crumb them, fry a golden brown in boiling fat or butter. Lay them on a sieve to drain off any fat there may be. Serve neatly on a dish, and decorate with fried bread and parsley.

---

10. Oyster Cutlets.

Stew one dozen oysters in their own liquor gently, till tender enough to chop very small; mix with them one cup of bread crumbs, some grated nutmeg and lemon peel, salt and pepper to taste; bind all together with a well-beaten egg or two, form into cutlets, and fry in butter a pale yellow;

drain on a sieve. Serve with fried sippets of bread and parsley round them. These are very delicious and simple.

---

11. Oysters Fried on Toast.

Take as many oysters as you need, dip each into well beaten egg, and then into bread crumbs, fry in butter a golden colour, sprinkle with pepper and salt.

Have ready as many pieces of fried bread, cut out with a round cutter, as you have oysters, lay an oyster on each ; garnish the top with a sprinkling of chopped green parsley and a piece or two of lemon cut in dice shape.

---

12. Irish Cutlets.

Remove the skin and bone from any cold fish you may have remaining ; well pound the flesh in a mortar ; add one cup of bread crumbs, salt and Nepaul pepper to taste, a teaspoon of chopped onion, a teaspoon of chopped parsley, mix all well together with one or two well beaten eggs, shape into cutlets, sausages, or rounds, and fry a pale golden colour.

Serve neatly garnished with parsley, and slices of lemon on a stand of potato.

---

13. Smoked Haddock Croquets.

Get a good sized smoked haddock, put it in the oven a few minutes, pick out all bones and skin, pound the flesh in a mortar, add one teaspoon chopped onion, one teaspoon of herbs as for veal stuffing, the grated rind of half a lemon, pepper and salt to taste, one teacup of fine bread crumbs ; mix well, bind all with one or two well beaten eggs, form into croquets, egg and bread crumb them, fry in butter a delicate gold colour. Serve round a wall of mashed potatoes; garnish with parsley and fried bread.

---

14. Baked Fish.

Get a good sized gurnet, stuff it with the following mixture ; tie it carefully round with tape (string cuts the fish), put it in a baking tin, cover over with little dotes of butter here and there and a sprinkling of salt and pepper. Put it into the oven, and bake till well done ; remove the tape carefully, so as not to spoil the look of the fish. Ornament with tufts of parsley, and serve with a dish of mashed potatoes, or fried potato chips.

Fish Stuffing.

One cup of fine bread crumbs, three ounces of butter well worked in, one teaspoon of herbs, as for veal stuffing, pepper and salt to taste, the yolks of two eggs. Mix all well together, and stuff the fish neatly.

---

15. Baked Smoked Haddock.

Get a good sized haddock, stuff it with the following mixture, and proceed as in above recipe.

Fish Stuffing.

One teacup of fine bread crumbs, two well boiled onions chopped and mashed to pulp, three ounces of butter, a small quantity of sage to taste chopped *very* fine, pepper and salt to taste. Mix all well together, and stuff the fish.

16. Curried Haddock.

Put a smoked haddock in the oven for a few minutes; free it of bone and skin and set it aside.

Cut up an onion very small, also two beads of garlic chopped, two bay-leaves chopped; fry in three ounces of butter with twenty-four cloves a nice brown, then add one tablespoon of best currie powder; stir; and, lastly, add the fish. Stir well, and keep frying till the fish is almost dry. Serve with a separate dish of plain boiled rice.

---

17. Curried Lobster.

Cut up an onion, two beads of garlic, two bay-leaves, and fry, in two ounces of butter with twenty-four cloves, a nice colour, then add one tablespoon of best currie powder. Let it all fry for two or three minutes, then add two table-spoons of tomato pulp, a blade of mace, and a cup of water; let it simmer gently for one hour, then just before serving add salt to taste, and a squeeze of lemon, and the contents of a best brand tin of lobster. Serve with a separate dish of boiled rice.

18. Curried Eel.

Cut up an onion, two heads of garlic, two bay-leaves, and fry in two ounces of butter and twenty-four cloves a nice brown; then add one tablespoon or a little less of best currie powder; stir; then add one cup of water, and a two-penny packet of Edwards' Tomato Soup. Let it simmer gently for one hour. Then add one pound of eels that have been nicely skinned and cleaned. Let the fish thoroughly cook in the sauce, and about five minutes before it is ready add the milk of a cocoanut. Serve with a dish of plain boiled rice.

---

19. Devilled Eels.

Well clean and skin one pound of eels, cut into two-inch lengths, roll in flour, sprinkle well with salt and Nepaul pepper. Fry in butter a nice colour. Serve, neatly heaped one on the other, with bits of parsley in between. Fried or mashed potatoes is the right accompaniment for this dish, or plain boiled rice.

20. Fish and Potato Cutlets.

Mash some potatoes, take any cold fish, free it of skin and bone. Mix them together with one teaspoon of chopped onion, one teaspoon of herbs as for veal stuffing, salt and pepper to taste, the grated rind of half a lemon. Form into cutlet shape, egg and bread crumb them, and fry a nice golden brown. Decorate with fried parsley.

----

21. Filleted Hake.

Get one pound of filleted hake. Chop up an onion very small, mix with a teaspoon of herbs, chopped parsley, lemon thyme and basil, and pepper and salt to taste. Sprinkle each fillet with this rather thickly, then roll it up and tie with a tape. Now put it aside. Cut up an onion, two beads of garlic, two bay-leaves, fry in two ounces of butter a nice yellow, then add one teacup of water and one packet Edwards' Tomato Soup. Let it simmer gently twenty minutes. Add your fillets, and let them cook in the sauce. Before serving untie the tape with great care.

22. Filleted Herrings.

Bake as many hard solid herrings as you require in vinegar, with a pinch of Nepaul pepper and salt, and two or three bay-leaves. When done, split each fish down the back, remove the bone, and then sprinkle with some chopped onion and green parsley, and put it together so that it looks as before. Serve cold, with a nice sauce made of equal parts of olive oil and vinegar. This is very nice served with salads of any kind.

---

23. Filleted Skate.

Get one pound of fillets of skate or crimped skate. Sprinkle them with a little chopped onion, parsley and a hard boiled egg chopped ; pepper and salt to taste. Roll the fish up, and tie with tape.

Cut up an onion into rings, chop two beads of garlic and fry in two ounces of butter a nice brown. Add two tablespoons of tomato pulp, one teacup of water, twelve cloves, twelve peppercorns, and two bay-leaves. Let it simmer gently half an hour, then add the skate, and cook it in

the sauce. Before serving, remove the tape and the bay
leaves.

-----

2 . Baked Mackerel.

Get some fine mackerel, sprinkle it over with Nepaul
pepper and salt, chopped onion, two bay-leaves, two beads
of garlic chopped fine, then pour over all one cup of tomato
pulp. Bake in the oven till the fish is done. Dish the fish
very neatly, and strain the liquor over them.

-----

25. Cod Steak.

Take some good sized pieces of cod, but not too large,
roll them in flour and fry a nice colour. Then fry some
onions as for beef steak, and smother the fish with them.

This is liked very much by children.

26. Curried Cutlets.

Free some cold haddock of bone and skin. Pound the flesh in a mortar. Mix with it one dessertspoon of chopped onion, two beads of chopped garlic, one teaspoon of best currie powder. Mix well. If not quite sufficiently firm to handle, stir in a well beaten egg. Form into cutlets, and fry in butter a nice colour. Serve with a separate dish of plain boiled rice or as a kedgree, as per recipe given.

---

27. White Cutlets.

Well pound any cold white fish you may have in a mortar. Add the grated peel of half a lemon, half a nutmeg grated, pepper and salt to taste. Mix well. Then add a well-beaten egg to bind the mixture, form into cutlets or flat cakes, and poach in milk till set. Serve with shrimp sauce over.

---

28. Fish and Tomatoes.

Get some red or grey mullet. Plain boil, and serve them in the middle of the dish. While hot melt some butter over them, and sprinkle with pepper and salt. Then surround them with small baked tomatoes all round the dish. Sprinkle over all some finely chopped parsley. Serve with potato snow.

---

29. Fish Mould.

Well pound the flesh of some nice white fish. Mix with it one cup of bread crumbs, one teaspoon of herbs as for veal stuffing, three ounces of butter, the grated rind of half a lemon, some grated nutmeg, Nepaul pepper and salt to taste. Well beat four eggs. Mix all together, put in a plain buttered mould, and bake till set. Turn out on to a paper. Garnish with parsley and slices of lemon and tomato.

---

30. Lobster Mould.

Well pound the contents of a tin of lobsters. Mix with one cup of bread crumbs, one teaspoon of herbs, the grated peel of half a lemon, some grated nutmeg, pepper and salt to taste, three ounces of butter. Well beat three eggs. Mix together, and put into a plain well-buttered mould. Steam till quite set. Turn out on to a round dish. Pour over a shrimp sauce.

N.B. —I have always said butter for all my fish dishes, as the butter imparts a better flavour, and in these days it can be had so cheaply; but if lard and dripping is substituted by those who do not object to their use, it answers quite as well.

EGGS IN VARIOUS WAYS.

1. Tumbled Eggs.

Put on half a pint of milk, with a piece of butter the size of a walnut. Well beat up four eggs, add one teaspoon of finely chopped onion, a little Nepaul pepper and salt to taste. Stir into the milk; keep stirring all the time till it gets thick. Then lay it on nicely buttered toast, and serve neatly dished and decorated with parsley.

2. Baked Eggs.

Well grease a pie dish. Break into it as many eggs as you require, taking care not to break the yolks. Sprinkle over the top a light layer of bread crumbs, and pepper and salt to taste. Put some dabs of butter here and there over

47

it, and bake a nice golden colour.   This dish, though simple, is tasty and satisfying.

---

3. Fricasseed Eggs.

Have ready some hard-boiled eggs.   Shell them, and cut them in quarters.   Place them in a dish neatly.   Now throw over them a white butter sauce, as per sauce recipe No. 1.   Sprinkle over some Nepaul pepper and salt to taste. These should be eaten with toast sent to table separately.

---

4. Dry Egg Currie.

Chop four hard-boiled eggs very fine.   Put them aside. Chop up one onion, two beads of garlic, very fine.   Fry in three ounces of butter, with twelve cloves, a nice brown. Then add a tablespoon of best currie powder.   Fry all together a few minutes, and then add the minced eggs. Stir well, and let all the moisture absorb. Add salt to taste, and a squeeze of lemon juice. Serve with a separate dish of boiled rice or kedgree, as per recipe given.

5. White Egg Currie.

Have ready some hard-boiled eggs; shell them and cut them in half. Put them aside. Chop one onion and two cloves of garlic small, and fry in three ounces of butter with twenty-four cloves a pale yellow, then add one dessert-spoon of the best currie powder, the milk of a cocoanut, and one small teacup of rich thick cream. Let it simmer gently for about half an hour. Strain it, and then add salt to taste, a squeeze of lemon, taking great care not to curdle the cream, and lastly, add the eggs. Warm thoroughly through. Serve with a separate dish of rice.

6. Egg Zeste.

Chop up six hard-boiled eggs small. Mix with them one teaspoon of chopped onions, one teaspoon of chopped parsley,

D

one bead of garlic, *very* fine, Nepaul pepper and salt to
taste, the grated rind of a small lemon, and lastly, the
strained juice of the lemon. This is very nice eaten with
salads of any kind, or between bread and butter as a
sandwich.

---

7. Baked Eggs with Cheese.

Butter a pie dish, sprinkle it well over with grated Parmesan cheese, a dust of Nepaul pepper and salt. Now
break in six eggs, cover over with grated cheese, a dust of
Nepaul pepper and salt, and bake a nice golden brown.

---

8. Plain Omelette.

Beat up the yolks of three eggs with two ounces of butter
quite smooth. Add to it pepper and salt to taste, and a
tablespoon of milk. Now beat the whites to a stiff froth,
and stir them thoroughly into the mixture. Put in just a
small pat of butter into a thoroughly clean frying-pan.
Pour in your mixture, and let it set and get a bright golden
yellow. Turn over neatly, lay it in a napkin, and garnish
with parsley. The chief secret is a clean pan and a perfectly clear fire, which must not be too fierce.

9. Omelette with Herbs.

Just as previous one. Only add to the mixture one teaspoon of chopped onion, and one teaspoon of parsley. Fry the same as above, and serve on a napkin.

---

10. Eggs with Tomatoes.

Well butter as many Darrol moulds (plain ones) as you require, break an egg into each, carefully, add a dust of pepper and salt, put a wee dab of butter on top, and bake in the oven till nicely set. Have ready as many nice round red tomatoes as you have eggs, put them in a greased baking-tin, put a small dab of butter on each, dust them with pepper and salt, and bake them till soft. Now dish with an egg and a tomato alternately, and sprinkle over all some chopped parsley. This is a simple but pretty and tasty dish.

---

11. Egg and Mushroom Souffle.

Boil one ounce of semolina in one cup of milk till quite thick, take it off the fire, stir into it while hot a piece of butter the size of a walnut; let it get cool. When nearly cold, stir in three well beaten eggs, yolks and whites

separately, the whites beaten to a stiff froth. Add Nepaul
pepper and salt to taste. Well butter a plain border
mould, fill the mixture in, let it bake till well set and of a
nice colour. Have ready some mushrooms, prepared thus—
pick and skin them, and fry them in plenty of butter, and
pepper and salt, till quite soft and done. Turn out your
soufflé on to a paper, and fill in the centre with the fried
mushrooms; sprinkle over the whole a little chopped
parsley. Serve very hot.

12. Egg Balls.

Boil some eggs hard, take out the yolks, pound them in a
mortar, mix with equal proportion of fine bread crumbs
passed through a wire sieve, add a teaspoon of fine chopped
onion, one bead of garlic, one teaspoon of parsley, one ounce
of butter; mix well; bind the mixture with well beaten raw
egg, form into balls, fry a nice brown, and serve strung on
skewers.

13. Egg Cutlets.

Chop some hard-boiled eggs fine. Mix them with an
equal quantity of fine bread crumbs. Add pepper and salt
to taste. Bind the mixture with well beaten raw eggs.
Form into nice shaped cutlets, and fry in butter a bright
golden yellow. Serve neatly, and garnish with fried parsley
and sippets of bread.

14. Surprise Eggs.

Boil as many eggs as you need hard. Cut a very small piece off the pointed end, so that the egg can stand, and then cut off as little as possible of the end—just enough to be able to take out the yolk nicely. If the white is very thick, thin it with a sharp knife, but be *very* careful not to spoil the shape. Pound the yolks in a mortar. Mix with them one or two anchovies also pounded, a bit of butter, some Nepaul pepper, a few fine bread crumbs. Mix well together, form the mixture into little balls, and proceed to fill the whites of the eggs, so that it looks somewhat like the yolk inside. Now have ready a nice salad made of lettuce, endive, tarragon, and chervil, chopped very fine, and looking like a bed of moss. On this set the eggs, and ornament with chopped beetroot. This is a very pretty dish, and exceedingly tasty, and suitable for breakfast, lunch, or dinner.

15. Stewed Eggs.

Have a nice, tasty brown sauce, as No. 17. Put to it as many hard-boiled eggs as you want, cut in half some turned olives, and a few button mushrooms. Let it warm thoroughly through, and serve, ornamented with fried sippets of bread.

LENTILS, RICE, AND MACARONI IN VARIOUS WAYS.

1. Lentil Moulds.

Boil half a pint of lentils in one pint of water till quite soft and mashed up; if more water is required, add a little drop; chop up an onion very small, two beads of garlic chopped, a pinch of lemon thyme, the grated rind of half a lemon, two eggs well beaten, pepper and salt to taste. Mix well together, butter some plain Darrol moulds, put the mixture in and bake till set, turn them out on to a paper, garnish with parsley, sippets of fried bread and hard-boiled eggs in quarters.

2. Lentil Cutlets.

Boil some lentils as in previous recipe, flavour in the same way, mix with them one teacup of bread crumbs, form into cutlets, fry in butter a nice colour. Dish neatly, and pour over them a tomato sauce, as per recipe No. 15.

3. Plain Dhàl.

Boil some lentils plain, put them aside, now cut up an onion, two beads of garlic, and fry in three ounces of butter with twenty-four cloves a pale yellow, then put in your lentils, and two bay-leaves. Let it simmer gently for about one hour; the lentils must not be thick; salt to taste. Serve with a separate dish of plain boiled rice, and slices of lemon, to squeeze over it.

4. Lentil Currie.

Boil some lentils plain, put them aside. Now cut up an onion, two beads of garlic, and two bay-leaves; fry in three ounces of butter with twenty-four cloves a nice brown, then add one tablespoon of the best currie powder, stir, and then put in your lentils; let them simmer gently for one hour; add salt to taste, and a small cup of tomato pulp. Serve with a separate dish of plain boiled rice.

5. Haricot Bean Pie.

Boil one pint of haricot beans till quite soft, put a mite of soda in the water to soften it, when quite done drain and set aside.

Cut up an onion into rings, chop up two beads of garlic; fry these in three ounces of butter with twenty-four cloves a nice golden colour. Now add one teaspoon of the best currie powder, and one cup of tomato pulp. Mix well, then add Nepaul pepper and salt to taste, a few drops of tarragon vinegar; put in your beans, and mix well. Turn out in a pie dish, and let them cool. Cover with a nice homely short crust, and bake a nice golden brown. This pie is nutritious, and really nice.

----

6. Haricot Bean Stew.

Boil one pint of beans till quite soft, drain, and set them aside. Make a thorough tasty brown sauce, as Nos. 16 or 18 in recipes given; pour it over the beans, warm all thoroughly through, and serve decorated with sippets of fried bread and slices of lemon.

----

7. Haricot Bean Currie.

Boil the beans as in previous recipe; cut up an onion and two beads of garlic; fry in three ounces of butter with twenty-four cloves a nice brown. Add one tablespoon of best currie powder, one cup of tomato pulp, a stick of cinnamon, a blade of mace, the peel of half a lemon grated, salt to taste; put in your beans, and let them simmer very gently for half an hour, taking great care they do not burn. Serve with a separate dish of rice.

---

8. Haricot Bean Pudding.

Get one pint of dried green haricots, boil till quite soft; mash them up thoroughly with a fork. Add three ounces of butter, pepper and salt to taste, one teaspoon of chopped parsley, one teaspoon of chopped onion; mix well. Add a well-beaten egg; well butter a plain mould; put the mixture in and steam for one hour. Turn out on to a dish, paper and decorate with parsley and small sliced tomatoes.

---

9. Plain Boiled Rice.

In boiling rice as it should be done, observe the following directions, and success is bound to follow :—(1) Use the best rice only. (2) Do not be afraid of plenty of water, four quarts to one pound. (3) Put in the rice as the water comes to the boil, having put in a good teaspoon of salt before you add the rice. (4) Watch carefully the *moment* the rice is soft, drain *at once* and set before the fire to steam for about half an hour or more; by this means your rice will be grain from grain separate, and look most appetising. These remarks apply to the cooking of rice in every form, when it is required dry, and to eat with savouries.

10. Yellow Rice.

Never throw away the water in which kedgrees or yellow
rice have been boiled. They make delicious soups on meat
days, with the addition of a little Armour's Beef Extract,
as the stock is already flavoured and thickened; or it will
make a delicious mullagatawny soup with the addition of
currie powder, and made according to recipe No. 9 (Soups),
without the herrings, and using the liquor instead. This
applies equally to the water in which haricot beans and
peas have been boiled. It always makes good stock for
soup.

Boil in the water you put on for your rice one large
onion whole, three beads of garlic whole, twenty-
four cloves, the seeds of twelve cardamoms, three
bay-leaves, two sticks of cinnamon, two blades of
mace, and a pennyworth of saffron, one heaped up teaspoon of salt. Let these come to the boil, and then
add one pound of the best rice. Watch carefully. Taste
it from time to time. The moment the rice is soft drain
at once, and set before the fire to steam. Before serving
remove the onion, garlic, bay-leaves, cinnamon, and mace,
but *not* the cloves and cardamoms. Decorate with onions
fried crisp and brown, sultanas fried, and almonds blanched
and fried. This is very nice.

11. Kedgree.

Put on some water with all the flavourings of the previous recipe, omit the saffron. When it comes to the boil add half a pound of pink lentils that have been well washed. When these change colour and get yellow, which will take about five minutes, add half a pound of best rice; stir well, and watch carefully. The moment the rice is done enough drain at once, and set before the fire to steam. Remove the spices, etc., as before, and decorate in the same way.

---

12. Another Kedgree.

Do some rice as yellow rice recipe. Add to it some flaked smoked haddock, and one teaspoon of herbs as for veal stuffing, and two ounces of butter. Mix well loosely with a fork. Serve hot, and decorate with hard-boiled eggs cut in quarters, and onions fried crisp and brown.

---

13. Another Kedgree.

The same as No. 11. Add to it four hard-boiled eggs chopped fine, two ounces of butter. Mix well lightly with a fork, and serve, decorated in the usual way with fried onions brown and crisp and fried almonds.

14. Tomato Rice.

Cut up an onion into thin rings, chop two beads of garlic, also two bay-leaves; fry this in three ounces of butter with twenty-four cloves a nice pale yellow. Now add one cup of tomato pulp, salt and Nepaul pepper to taste, a few drops of tarragon vinegar. Stir well; let it simmer for about twenty minutes; strain, and pour the sauce over some cold rice you may have by you; cover up, and warm thoroughly through. Serve decorated with bright West Indian pickles.

15. Cheese Pillau.

Boil some rice, with all the flavouring as for "yellow rice." Remove the spices, etc. Add two ounces of butter and three ounces of grated Parmesan cheese, Nepaul pepper and salt to taste. Mix all lightly with a fork. Dish garnished with watercress.

16. Rice Savoury.

Any cold rice you may have by you may do for this dish. Well beat up two eggs with a little milk; mix with one small onion chopped, one small bead of garlic, one teaspoon of chopped parsley, one teaspoon mixed of lemon thyme, tarragon and chervil, Nepaul pepper and salt to taste. Mix all well together. Put it into a plain mould well buttered ; put it in the oven till well set. Turn out on to a paper, Garnish with tufts of parsley and small red tomatoes.

———

N. B.—Rice can be cooked any colour, by simply adding a harmless vegetable colouring to the water in which it is boiled, and thus it looks very pretty served with stewed fruits, etc., as it makes the simplest thing look appetising and nice. Any cook with very little ingenuity could turn out any number of pretty and tasty dishes of rice alone ; it has the advantage of being nutritious and digestible, and is about the most economical thing there is in the market.

———

17. Macaroni Savoury.

Boil as much macaroni as you require, in salt and water. When tender, drain, and put it aside.

Cut up au onion into very thin rings, chop two beads of garlic small, fry in three ounces of butter with twenty-four cloves a pale yellow, then add one cup of tomato pulp; stir well ; the grated rind of half a lemon, Nepaul pepper and

salt to taste, a few drops of tarragon vinegar; pour over
the macaroni, and warm thoroughly through. This is a
delicious and most digestible dish. Garnish with watercress in bunches round the dish, and serve.

---

18. Macaroni Cheese.

Boil some macaroni plain. Put it in a well-buttered pie
dish thus—a layer of macaroni, a layer of grated Parmesan
cheese, a sprinkling of mustard and salt, till the dish is full
on the top, sprinkle the cheese. Beat up three eggs well in
one pint of milk, pour it over the macaroni, and well cover
it. Put a few dabs of butter over it here and there, and
put it in the oven, and bake a bright golden brown. Serve,
decorated with a nice frill round the dish.

---

19. Curried Macaroni.

Boil some macaroni. Put it aside. Cut up an onion into
thin rings, chop up two beads of garlic, fry in three ounces
of butter with twenty-four cloves a delicate brown. Now
add one tablespoon of best currie powder, one cup of tomato
pulp, the grated rind of half a lemon, and the strained juice
of half a lemon, salt to taste. Pour the sauce over the
macaroni, and serve thoroughly hot.

20. Macaroni Savoury.

Boil some macaroni, cut it into short lengths of about two inches long, well beat up three eggs. Mix with them one teaspoon of chopped onion, one teaspoon of herbs as for veal stuffing, one teaspoon of chopped parsley, Nepaul pepper and salt to taste. Mix it thoroughly with one cup of milk, and stir it well into the macaroni. Pour it into a pie dish, put a few dabs of butter over the top here and there, and bake a nice brown.

N.B.—Vermicelli answers all the same purpose as macaroni. Some like it better and think it more delicate ; both are cheap and nutritious, and both are capable of manipulation in a great many ways.

VEGETABLES IN VARIOUS WAYS.

1. Potato Baskets.

Get some nice long kidney potatoes, peel them very thin, cut them in half, then cut off a small piece at each end, so that the potato will stand like a cup, scoop out the inside neatly, leaving a thin wall of potato. Make it nice and smooth outside and in. Fry these in a bath of boiling fat a nice golden brown. Now take them out and stand them up like cups, fill each one with a farce of fish, or lentils, or mushrooms as desired, and sprinkle over the top some chopped parsley. This is a novel and pretty dish.

2. Potato Balls.

Boil some potatoes, pass them through a sieve. Mix with them some butter, pepper and salt, form into good sized balls with the hand, put them on a buttered tin, brush over them a well beaten egg, and put them in the oven till they are a nice brown colour.

3. Mashed Potatoes.

Mash some potatoes with butter, pepper and salt. Now well grease a plain pudding mould, fill your potatoes into it to get moulded, warm one minute, and turn out on to a dish, brush it over with well beaten egg, and then well sprinkle with find bread crumbs, put on little dabs of butter all over it, and bake in the oven a bright golden colour. Garnish with parsley.

---

4. Potato Snow.

Boil some potatoes, mash them with butter, pepper and salt, pass them through a wire sieve in the dish in which they are to be served. They must not be disturbed afterwards, as the light look would be gone, and so the dish get spoiled.

---

5. Potato Rings.

Well wash and thinly peel some nice large potatoes, cut them in slices, then take a nice cutter and stamp them out quite round, and then a smaller cutter to stamp out the centre so as to form a ring. Fry these rings a golden brown in a bath of fat, drain them in a sieve. Serve neatly dished and garnished with parsley. The centres need not be wasted, but fried for another dish.

E

6. Potato Pie.

Parboil some potatoes, slice them, put them in a pie dish thus—a layer of potatoes, then sliced onions and tomatoes, a few cloves, pepper and salt, and a spoonful of water, and so on till the dish is full. Cover with a light crust, and bake a golden brown, ornament with a frill round the dish, and serve.

7. Mixed Vegetable Pie.

Parboil some potatoes, carrots, turnips, some green cabbage, cauliflower. Cut the former into nice slices, the cauliflower into nice bunches, so, too, the cabbage. Now put them in a pie dish thus—a layer of the vegetable mixture, then some sliced onions and tomatoes and a few cloves and a spoonful of water, pepper and salt to taste; fill up the dish thus. Cover with a nice light crust and bake a golden brown ; ornament as before.

8. Stewed Onions White.

Parboil some onions (Spanish), put them aside. Have ready some white butter sauce, as recipe No. 1, and put

your onions into it, and finish cooking them in the sauce.
Serve with a sprinkling of pepper and salt over them.

---

9. Stewed Onions Brown.

Parboil some onions as before. Have ready a good brown
sauce, as recipe No. 14, put your onions in, and let them
finish cooking in the sauce. If liked, a sprinkling of chopped
parsley may be put over the onions before serving.

---

10. Farced Cucumbers Stewed.

Parboil some small cucumbers, scoop out the inside with
care, taking care the outsides are not injured. Stuff these
with a lentil farce, as recipe No. 1 for lentil moulds.
Have ready some good brown sauce as recipe No. 14, and
finish cooking your cucumbers in it. Dish neatly, and pour
the sauce round.

---

11. Cucumbers on Toast.

Boil some cucumbers (small ones) till tender. Lay them
neatly on pieces of toast, pour over them a white butter
sauce, as recipe No. 1. Sprinkle over with pepper and
salt, and serve hot.

12. Stewed Vegetable Marrow.

Get some small marrows, peel them, scoop out the inside carefully, stuff them with a farce thus—boil some onions, mash them with a fork. Add one cup of fine bread crumbs, some chopped sage to taste, two ounces of butter, pepper and salt. Mix well, and stuff the marrows. Now steam the marrows till nearly done. Have ready some good brown sauce, as recipe No. 14, finish cooking your marrows in that. Dish neatly, and pour the sauce round them. A separate boat of apple sauce to eat with them is liked by some.

13. Marrows on Toast.

Peel and cut into quarters some nice young marrows. Put the pieces into a jar with some butter, pepper and salt. Cover the jar close, and put it into the oven. Let the marrows cook in their own steam. When done place them on nicely cut pieces of buttered toast; sprinkle over them pepper and salt. These are really delicious.

14. Stewed Cabbage Stalks.

Get good thick stalks ; cut away all the outside, till you come to the tender part inside ; cut these into two-inch lengths. Parboil them in a little salt and water, and then finish cooking them, in either a white sauce as No. 1 recipe, or brown as No. 14 recipe. Either way they are truly delicious, and by far the best part of the cabbage in flavour and goodness.

---

15. Spinach with Eggs.

Well pick and wash some spinach ; put it in a pan with only the water that is in the leaves; let it boil till quite tender. Mash it with a fork with a little butter, pepper and salt. Put some on pieces of neatly cut buttered toast, then on each piece lay a well poached egg. Sprinkle over with pepper and salt, and serve.

---

16. Spinach Indian Way.

Wash and cook some spinach as before. Put it aside. Cut up an onion into rings, and fry in two ounces of butter a pale yellow. Put in your spinach ; stir well : add Nepaul pepper and salt to taste. This may be eaten on toast, or with plain boiled rice.

17. Farced Parsnips.

Parboil some nice young parsnips. Scoop out the inside, and stuff with a farce of fish made thus—boil a salt haddock, remove all skin and bone, pound the flesh in a mortar. Add one teaspoon of herbs as for veal stuffing, Nepaul pepper to taste, a small cup of bread crumbs, some butter and a teaspoon of chopped onions; bind the whole with well beaten eggs, and stuff your parsnips. Now finish cooking by steaming them. Serve neatly on a dish, and pour over them either a brown sauce as No. 14, or white as No. 1, whichever is liked best.

18. Farced Carrots.

Parboil some nice sized carrots. Scoop out the inside, and stuff with a farce as for lentil moulds, recipe No. 1. Finish cooking by steaming them, and then pour over a tomato sauce, as recipe No. 15, and serve.

19. Vegetable Stew.

Cut up an onion into rings, chop two beads of garlic, and fry in three ounces of butter with twenty-four cloves; let it get a nice golden colour. Now add sliced potatoes, carrots, turnips, parsnips, and pour over all one pint of water, two tablespoons of mushroom ketchup, salt and Nepaul pepper to taste. Cook till the vegetables are quite tender, and serve. This is quite as nice as Irish stew with meat in it.

20. Farced Tomatoes.

Scoop out the middle of the tomato with great care. Put into it a farce made thus—one small cup of bread crumbs, one teaspoon of herbs as for veal stuffing, two ounces of butter, pepper and salt to taste; bind with the yolk of one or two well beaten eggs. Stuff your tomatoes, put a little dab of butter on the top of each, sprinkle with pepper and salt, and bake in the oven till soft. Dish neatly; sprinkle over them some chopped green parsley. These may be served on pieces of fried bread. They are very nice served thus.

21. Mushroom and Olive Stew.

Make a nice brown sauce as recipe No. 14. Add to it some turned olives, and some nice button mushrooms. Garnish the dish with fried sippets of bread and chopped green parsley.

22. Mushrooms on Toast.

Well pick and clean some mushrooms, fry in about four ounces of butter, with pepper and salt to taste. Cook till the mushrooms get quite black. Serve on neatly cut pieces of toast; heap them one on the other, and garnish with tufts of parsley.

23. Celery Stew.

Cut up some nice tender stalks of celery into three-inch pieces, parboil in milk, then put it into a sauce as recipe No. 1, and finish cooking thus — add the grated rind of half a lemon, the grate of a nutmeg, Nepaul pepper and salt to taste. Lay this on nicely trimmed slices of toast, and serve. The celery may be stewed in a brown sauce, as per recipe No. 14, instead of the white; it is nice either way.

24. Sea-Kale Stew.

Serve the same as celery, or plain boil, and pour over a good white butter sauce, in which a little cream has been mixed, to make it extra rich.

25. Stewed Green Peas.

Shell your peas, and put them into a jar. Add two ounces of butter, a little pepper and salt, and one saltspoon of sugar; cover close, and put into the oven to cook in their own steam. When quite done, turn out into a dish, pour over them a good brown sauce, as No. 14, add a teaspoon of chopped green mint, and serve.

---

26. Stewed French Beans.

Get some tender French beans, cut them in two or three pieces each across, *not* lengthways, cook the same as peas in a jar, omitting the sugar. Turn out on a dish, and pour over them a brown parsley sauce, as recipe No. 18.

---

27. French Beans on Toast.

Get some very young French beans, put them in whole in a jar, with butter, pepper and salt, and a mite of soda to preserve the colour. Cook them as in previous recipe. Turn them out when done, and lay on neatly cut slices of well buttered toast. Sprinkle over with pepper and salt, and serve very hot.

28. Stewed Broad Beans.

Well boil some broad beans in salt and water; take off the skins, and pour over the beans a parsley and butter sauce, as recipe No. 3. These may be served on toast, and thus make a substantial dish, and very nice.

29. Jerusalem Artichokes on Toast.

Peel very carefully and trim nicely; throw them into cold water as you peel them, or they will get discoloured. Boil in salt and water till quite soft; drain; mash them with a fork till quite smooth, with butter, pepper and salt. Put the artichokes thickly on nicely cut pieces of buttered toast, and sprinkle with pepper and salt, and serve. This is simply delicious, though simple.

30. Egg Plant Savoury.

Cut up some egg plants into quarters; put them into a jar, with butter, pepper and salt; cover close, and put in the oven. When done, take them out, mash them smooth with a fork. Add two hard-boiled eggs chopped fine, and a few bread crumbs, fill the mixture with little scallop shells, brush over the top of each with well beaten egg, sprinkle on some fine bread crumbs, put a little dab of butter on each, and just put in the oven to brown. Serve them in the shells, neatly dished.

SALADS IN VARIOUS WAYS.

THESE are very little understood in this country. Almost any vegetable cold can be made into a most appetising salad. By this means you have really delicious dishes, and there is no waste of cold vegetables or fish. I will give a few which, though known, are very seldom used, and I want to impress the fact in the minds of my readers that salads are healthy and economical, and generally liked by young and old, and the very little trouble they take in preparation is well repaid by the result.

1. Potato Salad.

Mash up any cold potatoes you may have, mix them with any cold fish. Add a tablespoon of best olive oil, some caper vinegar, and a few chopped capers, one teaspoon of chopped onions, one bead of garlic chopped very small, the grated rind of a small lemon, the juice of half a lemon strained, salt and Nepaul pepper to taste; mix thoroughly. Serve it in a glass dish neatly piled up, smooth with a fork. Sprinkle over the whole some chopped hard-boiled egg, and arrange pretty West Indian pickles over it for decoration.

75

2. Plain Potato Salad.

Cut up any cold potatoes in slices, mix with them a tea-spoon of chopped onion, a teaspoon of chopped parsley, and pour over it equal quantities of best olive oil and vinegar that has been well mixed with a little pepper and salt.

3. Mixed Vegetable Salad.

Cold carrots, turnips, potatoes, green peas, French beans, beetroot, celery, cauliflower, etc. Cut the carrots, turnips, potatoes, etc., with a nice fancy vegetable cutter; mix in the green peas, the French beans cut up in two or three pieces each, the cauliflower in neat little branches. Mix with them a teaspoon of chopped onion, a teaspoon of chopped parsley; mix equal quantities of vinegar and best olive oil, with pepper and salt to taste; toss all lightly up together. Ornament with lettuce and watercress in bunches.

N.B.—German lentils, green peas, French beans, broad beans, all make a good salad by themselves with equal quantities of oil and vinegar, and pepper and salt. No cold vegetable is out of place.

Every one more or less knows how to make salads from

lettuce, endive, watercress, radishes, mustard and cress, etc., etc. ; so it would be useless to enter into that in this little book. I will, however, give directions for a few simple salad sauces that I find generally approved of.

4. Salad Sauce No. 1.

Boil some eggs hard, two or three will be enough, take out the yolks, bruise them with the back of a spoon quite smooth, add a teaspoon of made mustard. Mix well, then add two tablespoons of olive oil, a little at a time, till well mixed, then two tablespoons of vinegar, stirring all the while. Lastly, a few drops of tarragon vinegar, a few drops of garlic vinegar, a salt spoon of castor sugar, and salt to taste. Some like a spoonful of anchovy sauce added ; this is, of course, a matter of taste.

5. Sauce No. 2.

Break in the yolks of three eggs into a basin, stir with a wooden spoon, with two tablespoons of olive oil, but a drop at a time only till the egg gets thick ; then mix in two tablespoons of vinegar gradually, a few drops of tarragon, a few drops of garlic, a spoonful of made mustard, and, lastly, two tablespoons of cream, but this must be mixed with great care so that it does not curdle. Salt to taste.

6. Sauce No. 3.

One potato passed through a sieve, the hard-boiled yolk of one egg rubbed smooth, two tablespoons of olive oil, two tablespoons of vinegar, a few drops of tarragon vinegar, a few drops of garlic vinegar, and a few drops of Chili vinegar ; mix all well and smoothly. Add salt to taste.

N.B.—All salads should have a dash of onion and garlic, but very judiciously mixed. The difference in the flavour of the salads is very great.

Green salads may be mixed with lobsters, anchovies, sardines, and any kind of cold fish.

PUDDINGS AND SWEETS.

I FIND the generality of ordinary puddings are dreadfully insipid. It is not at all necessary that this should be the case. And flavouring is cheap enough. Appearance, too, is a great thing. The sense of sight, smell, and taste can easily enough be gratified with very little trouble. And when one takes into consideration that our health depends on the way in which our food is prepared, it becomes an actual matter of duty to take the necessary trouble to prepare it properly, and bringing both intelligence and taste to bear on the subject.

---

1. Currant and Apple Tart.

Make a nice short crust of Coombs' Eureka Flour, thus—half a pound of flour, three ounces of butter, one egg well beaten, a pinch of salt, and one teaspoon of castor sugar. Make it into a nice dough with milk. Put in a pie dish one layer of dry currants well washed and picked, a little grated lemon peel, and a few drops of lemon juice, then a spoonful of treacle and a few very fine bread crumbs, then a layer of sliced fresh apples, and again the currants, and so on till the dish is full. Cover with the paste rolled thin, and ornament prettily on the top with the paste nicely cut out, etc., etc. Bake a nice golden brown, and when a little cool sprinkle castor sugar over the top. Serve with a nice custard or cream.

2. Cabul Cassalettes.

Put half a pound of dried apricots to soak for about four hours, pour the water in which they have been soaked into an enamel saucepan, about a cupful. Add half a pound of sugar, a little grated lemon peel, and the juice of half a lemon. Let it get into a syrup, then add the fruit, and let it simmer gently for one hour. Make a nice puff paste of Coombs' Eureka Flour, roll out thin, and line some nice shaped patty pans, well greased, with the paste; prick it with a fork to prevent it blistering. Put it in a quick oven and bake a pretty golden brown, turn out of the pans, and fill the cases with the apricot stew; then *well* whip some cream very stiff, put it smoothly over the top of each, so that it looks like white foam, and then sprinkle over all either crushed crystallised violets or chopped pistachio nuts. Both are pretty, or do half with the violets and half with the nuts. Arrange them neatly in a glass dish, with a dish paper under. These are very pretty, and very delicious, and simple to make.

3. Fried Almond Rings.

Make a paste thus—half a pound of Coombs' Eureka
Flour, two ounces of butter, two ounces of sugar, a quarter
pound of almonds ground to a paste. Mix well together.
Add one well-beaten egg, with just enough milk to make
the mixture into a good dough, roll out about a quarter of
an inch thick, stamp out some rounds about the size of the
top of a tumbler, then take some smaller rounds and stamp
out the inside so as to form rings. Fry these rings in a
bath of boiling lard a pale golden colour, drain them on a
sieve, and sprinkle well over with castor sugar. Serve on
a dish paper neatly. The inner rounds may be put on a
well floured baking tin, and baked in the oven as biscuits.
So there need be no waste. They are nice both ways.

---

4. Digestible Plum Pudding.

Put one tablespoon of crushed loaf sugar into a pan.
Let it get quite brown, but do not let it burn. Add to it
one pint of hot milk ; stir well till the sugar dissolves in
the milk. Have ready three ounces of fine florador dissolved in enough milk to make it like thick cream; stir this
into the milk as it is on the point of boiling. Let it get
very thick ; stir in two ounces of fresh butter, quarter a
pound of sultanas washed and picked, quarter a pound of
currants washed and picked, two ounces of citron peel
chopped small, half a grated nutmeg, the grated rind of

F

half a lemon, two well beaten eggs; stir all well (but do
not put in the eggs till the pudding is a little cool, as they
will curdle), put it in a well greased plain mould, and steam
till well set and firm. Turn out on a dish, and ornament
with glacé cherries, angelica, etc., etc. This is a very
digestible plum pudding, and may be safely eaten by in-
valids, who dare not touch ordinary plum pudding. It is
in the opinion of some very much nicer than the usual
Christmas puddings.

5. Plain Florador Pudding.

Put one tablespoon of crushed loaf sugar into a pan.
Let it get brown, but do not let it burn, then add one pint
of hot milk. Have ready three ounces of fine florador
(semolina will do) mixed with enough milk to make it like
thick cream, stir it into the milk just as it comes to the
boil, let it thicken, then add two ounces of butter, a little
more sugar to taste, and any flavouring approved of. Turn
it into a pie dish, and bake in the oven a nice brown on
the top. Let it cool a little, and sprinkle over the top
some hundreds of thousands, and serve.

6. Boiled Banana Pudding.

Make a crust thus—a half pound of Coombs' Eureka Flour,
a pinch of salt, and a quarter pound of chopped suet. Mix

well with enough water to form it into a dough, roll out thin, line a plain well-greased pudding mould with the paste, and fill in thus—some nice ripe bananas cut in slices, a few cloves, the grated rind of half a lemon, the juice of one lemon strained, one tablespoon of castor sugar, a small cup of water. Cover over the top with paste, tie with a cloth wrung out of boiling water. Steam for about two hours. Turn out carefully, and serve with a nicely flavoured custard.

7. Banana Custard.

Well mash two bananas into a complete pulp. Put with one pint of milk and the well beaten yolks of three eggs sugar and vanilla flavouring to taste. Stir well. Put it into a pan, and put the pan into a larger one with boiling water in it. Stir all the time for twenty minutes, and pour it into custard cups. This is very delicious and novel.

8. Cocoanut Rice.

Boil a quarter pound of small rice in one pint of milk till quite soft. Then add two ounces of butter, sugar to taste, and three ounces of desiccated cocoanut. Stir well, and pour into a plain mould that has been rinsed with cold water. Let it get cold. Turn out of the mould into a glass dish, decorate with pretty sweets, such as those sold by Messrs. Clark Nicholls and Coombs, or Mr. E. Roberts of Camberwell.

---

9. Cocoanut Macaroni.

Boil half a pound of macaroni in water till tender, drain, put it in a pie dish. Mix with it a quarter pound of desiccated cocoanut. Well beat up two eggs with rather more than a half pint of milk, with sugar to taste. Pour it over the macaroni, and see that it is well covered. Put a little dab of butter here and there over it. Bake it in the oven a nice colour. Let it cool a little, and sprinkle castor sugar over it, or any pretty fruits.

Vermicelli will answer the purpose quite as well.

---

10. Cream Rolls.

Get as many nice plain, round, smooth, little rolls as you may require. Cut a little piece off the top of each with care; now scoop out the crumbs out of each with very great care, and also take off any crumbs there may be on the pieces cut off the tops. Well beat two eggs with about one cup of milk. Add a little sugar to taste. Put the custard in a bowl, dip each roll and the piece cut off in the custard, but not enough to moisten it so that it gets too soft. Now fry all of them in a bath of boiling lard a nice golden brown. Drain on a sieve. When cold, fill each one up thus—a little guava jelly at the bottom, and then cream whipped stiff and flavoured with a little sugar, the grated peel of half a lemon, and a little lemon juice. Then put on the top that was cut off, sprinkle over with castor sugar. Serve on a dish paper. These are delicious.

---

11. Semolina Cup Puddings.

Put on one pint of milk in the pan, with two ounces of fresh butter and sugar to taste, and some grated rind of lemon to taste. Have ready about three ounces of semolina mixed with enough milk to make it like thick cream. Pour it into the milk just as it comes to the boil; stir well, and let it get very thick. Pour into very small cups that have been rinsed in cold water. When cold, turn out in a glass dish, neatly, and pour over it a nicely flavoured custard, and grate over the top a little nutmeg. Each cup can be decorated with dried fruit if desired, but it is very simple and nice as it is.

---

12. Cream Cake Pudding.

Make a cake thus—one pound of Coombs' Eureka Flour, a quarter pound of sugar, a quarter pound of butter. Mix well together; add three well beaten eggs with enough milk to make the mixture like very thick whipped cream. Pour it into a well-buttered quite plain pudding mould (tin), bake a nice colour, let it stand about ten minutes, and then turn out. Next day scoop out all the inside, leaving a wall of cake about one and a half inches thick; fill this up as follows—a layer of strawberry jam, then a layer of thick cream, till it is filled up; cover the top with cream, and smooth with a wet palette knife ; decorate the top with two nice strawberry sweets in the middle, and some half moon almond paste sweets laid round the edges, either plain or interlaced, by putting a second round over the first, then stick three long pieces of angelica, and make a tripod handle This is pretty and nice.

13. Boiled Vermicelli Pudding.

Boil a quarter pound of Vermicelli in about half a pint of milk till soft, sweeten a little, then make a custard thus— two eggs well beaten, half a pint of milk, vanilla to taste, also a little castor sugar. Pour the custard over the vermicelli ; stir well together ; pour it into a mould that has been well greased. Steam for about one hour or more till quite set. Take great care in turning it out, as it is apt to break. Ornament with dried cherries cut in half, and chopped pistachio nuts, or with pretty sweets.

14. Florador Custard Pudding.

Boil one pint of milk. Have ready two ounces of fine florador, mixed with enough milk to make it like cream; stir this into the milk as it comes to the boil; let it thicken. Now take it off the fire; stir in two ounces of fresh butter, sugar and flavouring to taste. Well beat up three eggs, and when the florador is cooled a little, mix in the eggs with it. Pour into a pie dish, and bake in the oven till set and of a nice golden brown. When a little cool, sprinkle over the top a little castor sugar that has been made a pretty pink by adding a drop of cochineal to it in a dry state, and rubbing it with the fingers.

15. Orange Fritters.

Get two or three nice large oranges, peel them carefully so as not to break the inner part. Divide into skeins, and carefully take off all the white pithy part, but on no account break the skin. Make a batter thus—quarter pound of flour, the yolks of two raw eggs, one tablespoon of olive oil. Mix it with enough cold water to make it a stiff batter. Whip the whites of the eggs to a stiff froth, with a pinch of salt, and add this to the batter; stir and use; dip each skein of orange in it, and fry in a bath of boiling lard a nice golden brown; drain on a sieve. Serve on a dish paper, and sprinkle all over with castor sugar; better still, roll each skein in castor sugar. This is uncommon, and nice.

---

16. Pine Apple Sweet.

Put into a pan a quarter pound of butter, with a quarter pound of sugar, and two ounces of fine florador; stir well till it gets quite smooth, then add four slices of pine-apple that have been mashed to a complete pulp and passed through a sieve; add a spoonful or two of water, and let it cook till the florador is quite done and looks clear. Pour into a mould that has been rinsed in cold water. When quite cold, turn out with care in a glass dish, surround the dish with cream, nicely flavoured with pine-apple flavouring. Decorate with either dried fruits or pretty sweets.

---

17. Apple Sweet.

Exactly the same as the pine-apple, only using apples boiled and pulped instead. About four good sized apples will be needed, and the cream flavoured with lemon. Decorate in the same way, or with pink and white cocoanut chips.

18. Pumpkin Tart.

Make a puff paste of Coombs' Eureka Flour, and line a nice sized shallow tin pan with it. Grease the pan well; prick the paste to prevent it blistering; bake a nice colour and turn out of the pan. Fill up with a mixture made thus — boil one pound of nice ripe yellow pumpkin till soft; pass it through a sieve. Add to it half a pound of sugar, the grated rind of a small lemon, the strained juice of a lemon, the strained juice of an orange, a few cloves. Boil till it looks nice and clear; take out the cloves, and fill the mixture into the paste case. Cover over neatly with well whipped cream, and sprinkle over the top some chopped pistachio nuts.

19. Jerusalem Artichoke Jelly.

Nicely peel one and a half pounds of Jerusalem artichokes, and throw them into cold water as you do them, else they discolour. Boil them till soft; drain and mash them to a complete pulp. Add one pound of castor sugar, and boil till the artichokes get quite clear. Mix with them a good deal of vanilla flavouring to overcome the artichoke flavour; taste it so as to have it right; then put the mixture into a greased plain mould. Let it get cold before turning out;

dip it for one instant in very hot water so as to melt the grease, and turn out in a glass dish. Decorate with nice dried crystallised fruits. This is nice, and is nutritious.

20. Banana Pancakes.

Well mash two bananas to a pulp, mix up a quarter of a pound of flour, two eggs well beaten, yolks and whites separately, the whites to a froth; mix with enough milk to make a stiff batter. Add the bananas to it, and fry in lard or butter a golden brown; turn over neatly; drain on a sieve. Serve on a napkin or dish paper; sprinkle well over each some castor sugar. Serve with sliced lemon.

21. Coffee Cream Puddings.

Boil one pint of milk, have ready three ounces of fine florador mixed with just enough milk to make it like thick cream; stir it into the milk just as it comes to the boil, stir well till it gets very thick, stir into it two ounces of fresh butter, sugar to taste, and enough coffee essence to give it a good flavour, and a few drops of almond flavouring. Pour into small plain Darrol moulds that have been rinsed in water, let them get quite cold and set. Turn them out on a glass dish; put on the top of each a spoonful of thick whipped cream, and a glacé cherry in the middle.

———

22. Chocolate Cream Puddings.

The same as the last, but instead of coffee put in two ounces of *good* cocoa, flavour with vanilla, and decorate each little mould with pistachio nuts, blanched and cut in strips, and stick all over the little moulds like porcupine quills.

Cream may be served with these separately.

———

23. Sponge Cake and Banana Pudding.

Crumble up half a dozen sponge cakes, cover them with a custard made thus—two bananas mashed to a pulp, two eggs well beaten, one pint of milk, sugar to taste, and vanilla flavouring. Pour over the sponge cakes, stir well together, put over the top little dabs of butter here and there; bake a nice brown. Decorate with pink castor sugar sprinkled over the top.

---

24. Strawberry Cream Pudding.

Mix some cochineal with ordinary clear plain jelly ; line a plain mould with this. Let it set about a quarter of an inch thick, then fill up the mould with the following—half a pound of strawberriers passed through a sieve; mix with one cup of good thick cream, sugar to taste, and a little liquid jelly. Mix well together, and pour it in the lined mould. Let it get quite cold and set ; dip the mould into hot water for a second ; whip the water off, and turn out on a glass dish. Decorate with leaves and flowers of the strawberry.[1]

---

25. Hen's Nest Pudding.

Get some egg shape moulds, fill them with a mixture made as recipe No 11, only using fine florador instead of

[1] Raspberries can be done the same way.

semolina. When cold, turn in thus—cut into thin chips some pale lemon and orange peel, so as to resemble straw as much as possible. Take off all the sugar, put the chips in a glass dish (a round one is best), form them as much as possible like a nest, and lay the eggs in them. Serve with a nice custard in custard glasses separately. This is a pretty dish when well made. Some use jelly cut in strips instead of the peel, but it must be very carefully done to look nice.

26. Fancy Sweets.

One pound of Coombs' Eureka Flour, half a pound of sugar, half a pound of butter ; mix these well together, then add four eggs, yolks and whites separately, the whites beaten to a stiff froth ; mix with enough milk to make the consistence of stiff whipped cream. Take out a third of the mixture, and colour a nice pink with cochineal, and flavour with a few drops of almond essence, also put in a few blanched almonds cut in half; the rest of the mixture flavour with lemon, and put in some glacé cherries cut in half. Well butter a square and shallow cake tin, pour in half the plain mixture with cherries, let it spread and flatten, then pour the pink mixture on the top of that, let that also spread and flatten, and then pour the rest of the cherry mixture on the top; smooth with a wet knife and bake till set and a nice colour. Leave it for about ten minutes, and turn out. Let it get quite cold, then cut it into small squares; smooth the top of each by cutting it quite even. Then pour over each an icing made thus—half a pound of confectioners' sugar, with about two tablespoons of water, stir well; just let it boil up, and cover the tops of the cakes smoothly; then sprinkle over the top with pink chip cocoanut, hundreds of thousands, pistachio nuts, or crushed crystallised violets, each cake with a different decoration. This is a pretty dish, and very nice.

27. Sago Jelly.

Boil a quarter pound of small sago in one quart of water till quite clear and thick—if too thick add a little more water—but it must be very thick and stiff. Now add a half pound of sugar, the juice of three oranges strained, a drop or two of oil of oranges, a pennyworth of saffron that has been dissolved in a wine glass of boiling water and strained, some almonds blanched and cut into thin strips. Mix all well together, and pour into a plain mould that has been rinsed with cold water. Let it get quite cold and set, and turn out on a glass dish. Decorate with chow-chow according to fancy.

28. Sweet made of Bread.

Cut some slices of stale bread of a close texture, stamp it out in neat rounds, soak it in one egg well beaten in a small cup of milk, fry in lard a golden brown. Now cover over each any kind of jam that is liked best. Cover with whipped cream and ornament with a sprinkling of pink chip cocoanut, or to make it of two different colours the cream can be coloured with a few drops of cochineal, and ornament with white chip cocoanut. This is a very simple and pretty sweet.

29. Chestnut Souffle.

Boil about thirty chestnuts in water till soft. Remove the shell and outer skin; pound the nuts in a mortar with a few drops of orange flower water. Well beat the yolks of three eggs. Add them to the chestnuts with enough sugar and almond flavouring to taste. Stir into the paste about one pint of milk. Now beat the whites of the eggs to a stiff froth, and stir in gradually. Pour the mixture into a soufflé dish and bake a nice colour. Serve direct from the oven, as a soufflé falls in getting cold, and is spoilt.

30. Treacle Balls.

A half pound of Coombs' Eureka Flour, a pinch of salt, half a teaspoon of ginger powder, the grated rind of a small lemon, a quarter pound of treacle. Mix well together, add two well beaten eggs, form iuto small balls, and fry in a bath of boiling lard a golden brown. The balls will swell a little in cooking. Sprinkle well over with castor sugar, and serve.

THE END.

www.ingramcontent.com/pod-product-compliance
Lightning Source LLC
Chambersburg PA
CBHW021410090426
42742CB00009B/1089